BOOK of

Happiness

BOOK of Happiness

MAJA PANIC

iUniverse, Inc.
Bloomington

Book of Happiness

iUniverse books may be ordered through booksellers or by contacting:

iUniverse
1663 Liberty Drive
Bloomington, IN 47403
www.iuniverse.com
1-800-Authors (1-800-288-4677)

ISBN: 978-1-4759-6573-5 (sc)
ISBN: 978-1-4759-6574-2 (ebk)

Printed in the United States of America

iUniverse rev. date: 12/04/2012

A BOOK OF HAPPINESS

The pages which appear empty in this book are not really empty but partly filled with my positive energies making your way to a better and happier life easier, in every part of that way. The thing you have to do is very simple—you should just follow the very easy instructions throughout the book, to write, in the place indicated in the book, your intimate things and wishes and already after a very short time, without any additional effort, you will, start to convince yourself how easy is the solution of your seemingly unsolvable problems and by a method which is simpler and more successful than any hitherto known.

When solving your problems, as in using this specific book, be patient and use, every now and then, my photoes too in order to catch my positive nergy. This energy, as my present to you, will start, together with your crystal clear thoughts, the process of healing and realisation as well as solving the problems you are at the moment conftonted with.

Thius book doesn't just speak about hapiness it also acts as a strongest talisman, your amulet, powerful matter for bringing hapiness to your life.

Already when just reading the Book of Hapiness some things in your life will very obviously start to change, melting down the Negative and the Bad giving up, almost imperceptibly, its place to the good vibrations and happy circumstances.

Please try—get rid of doubts for as somebody said a long ago—the most difficult problems are solved by simplest means—only if you know how.

Good luck!

Please direct any of your remarks, praise or comment to the address MEAVITA Zagreb, Kriska 93, Croatia
or make an appoinment for an interview by phone 00 385 (0) 91 2888850
or e-mail meamaja@gmail.com.

BEFORE YOU START

Very probably you have already leafed through your Book of Hapiness and you were suprised by its simplicity and the number of empty pages. Already by taking this book in your hands, you have touched the fine and gentle vibrations directed to you only bringing a moment of peace and serenity to your thoughts.

Before starting to read further and before starting to work on yourself, be aware of the fact that you are not alone as we have already established our unique energy connection. Breathe deeply in and let the "heaviness" out. Thereafter apply yourself to your first step by filling in the following empty page describing what you feel and what is bothering you.

Don't think too much, let the words flow in and describe, shortly and clearly, your innermost situation.

_____

_____

_____

_____

_____

_____

_____

_____

_____

_____

_____

_____

_____

_____

_____

_____

_____

THE BOOK OF HAPPINESS

When you look at the world in a narrow way,
How narrow it seems!

When you look at it in a mean way,
How mean it is!

When you look at it selfishly,
How selfish it is!

But when you look at it in a broad, generous, friendly spirit,
What wonderful people you find in it!

Horace Rutledge

ABOUT THE AUTHOR

Maja Panic was born in Zagreb, in 1966, with the characteristics belonging to the charismatic people only—of course not in any physical sense but in a more subtle way. Although born in a family of highly educated and socially high positioned parents, she has very early started to deviate from the taditional forms of life, creating her own ways, never shrinking, not for a moment, from any problems as they arose, from every attempt to impose her personal expressive spirituality she radiated into his unmerciful and not a bit romantic times.

Already at her early age her ideas and standpoints in life were refused even by the ones who stood nearest to her as, of course, her standpoints were not based on logic and „sane mind". However, with years her more precise feelings and premonitions, unfortunately mostly of unhappy events regarding the people in her vicinity, started to become reality while her analyses of persons, events and various problems pointed to the presence of, at least, paranormal abilities.

At the first glance she seems to be a very ordinary woman, wife and mother who does not, in any way, put herself forward and seemingly blends in with her environment. She manages her world with her optimism and smiles, going bravely on, proud of her small achievments. The astonishing fact is that Maja when walking through her simple but very hard and difficult life, did not loose, not for a moment, her optimism and strength realising, persistently, her career of a charismatic, pulling people after her to a better world explaining all things unknown to a rational mind.

The great value of Maja's words, her energy and her natural abilities are everyday events. They raised her knowledge and skills on enviable heights desirable in every sphere of existence and today, with her 43 years of age, she is greatly respected by numerous thankful visitors, enjoying the role of destiny which presented her with her mysterious characteristics. Even now she is still benevolent, even naive, when speaking of material things in life; she keeps performing her mission and speaks about it very modestly when asked.

Very long ago Maja started to communicate with other types of intelligence for which many people are neither brave nor not open enough. These encounters open new visions for her and stimulate her energetic abilities. Her "tools" are dreams and visions and an unbelievable instinct when a person is stepping along a bad way. In her work she stresses the fact that the existence of higher spheres is approachable and open to all of us, only if we know how to direct our sincere wish—the success will not fail to appear. She told her experiences from long ago when she experienced spiritually very distant places and as she says—"There is enough sunlight for everyone and the way thereto must not be full of thorns."

Maja's objectives were never to succeed as an alchemist of the contemporary life and to develop theories on magic beliefs although she does practise some of such skills. Since some of these customs really do have their origin in ancient times, customs which really could protect one from danger and bad events—she offeres this to a mass of people who visited her hitherto and their repeated visits prove that her methods brought a ray of light to everyone of them during some moments in their life.

She also started to introduce the Tarot cards into her method using them in a very specific way in order to get the insight with some future events. The Tarot cards are hiding the soul of the world, mixed with its energies and interwoven with the symbols, hiding the secret messages coming from the Universum. One of the unwritten rules is that the cards choose themselves the person who will manage them and not the other way around . . . . Her cards (Mea Vita) and later her published book (Handbook for the Mea Vita Tarot Cards) got her a large number of followers exactly regarding this new way of how to use the Tarot cards. Her cards are benevolent, friendly and warning; they give its stamp to a hard destiny; they are here to show everybody that there is always a choice—not only to choose between a better of two evils but the choice to make something better of one's life.

"Nothing in life happens by accident"—Maja says often to her clients. When Maja was twentyone a special lady entered her life who introduced her to the world of the esoterics and secrets she did not know, in her early youth, how to manage. This was all destiny . . . —said Maja in one of her interviews. She transferred unselfishly her knowledge to me for she said that I have a potential, that I have a heart meant to help others. Years thereafter she was teaching me, opening door after door so that I may experience various events. One was my encounter with the so-called "Threshold Guardian"—meaning that one could, being fully conscious and aware, see, feel and speak with persons from other worlds of the endless Universum.

"I was even frightened at first but now I know that it was He, the Threshold Guardian—my spiritual leader, whom some people call their angel, their God . . ."

Maja works simply, for she is a simple person, always easygoing, easy to talk to, easy to communicate with, but, in spite of that, her every word leaves a very impressive and strong impact to whoever listens to her. In these moments her eyes are the mirrors of other people souls and worlds while the words she says are clean, sincere and valuable . . .

"When I feel the soul of the person I communicate with, whether this person is near or whether we communicate by a distance, I feel the beatings of her or his heart and pictures and films are simply unwinding themselves to me with this person playing the leading role . . ."

Sara Mikacic, prof.

INTRODUCTION

Why me? My wishes never come true . . . . Perhaps I am bewitched? Under a spell? What is waiting for me in the future? How to create the best ways of life? Will I have a husband, children? How to stop being unhappy? Will I get money? Maybe he doesn't love me? How long will it go on like that? Will I get better? . . . . All these are questions thousands of people think about every day and neither I can find an answer to these questions, nor can I give you an answer what is actually the meaning of life itself.

Although there are many situations in life when one may come to the conclusion that life is hard and merciless, haven't we, however, more than once been silent witnesses when wonders were created in the lives of some people who only recently suffered chaos and bad luck. Yes, there really are many cases when, instead of evil, people were touched by a strike of hapiness, the lucky ray of sun, seemingly sudden and without any cause whatsoever. There were never any scientific proofs as evidence that there exist some people and customs as well as some so-called regulations which may „push out" evil and make place for happiness of an individual. At the same time we are all aware of the fact that each and every such change for the better has an invisible and benevolent help. There really are people in existence who may help—but only if you yourself are not able to do so for a thing all of us have within reach ist strength of the Law of Universum which is at everybody's, but really everybody's, disposal through rare moments when some inexplainably strong reactions, conditioned by right guidelines, are happening, enriching with happiness the lives of some individuals.

Some people are more brave, more aware or more able than others, those rare ones who were able to bring their body, mind and spirit into harmony get, as a rule, more happiness in life, are more successful and healthier but also more open for quicker and easier realisation of great objectives in life. The others, not properly educated in the sense of events which cannot be explained by logic, or those who are weaker, go since centuries ago for help to healers, seers and similar who have a more expressive gift of observation and may thus transfer the message from the Universe.

After a number of years and too many people who visited me I decided to share a part of what I do in my direct contact with all those who are unhappy and dissatisfied with their lives in this way—through the BOOK OF HAPINESS in order to offer a possibility to everyone to remove the blockade and solve the problems they are confroted with through the life by himself or by herself. The area through which I act, officially called alternative, brought richness to my life in the sense of various persons and destinies while their life stories and problems, when taking over my energy, strenghtened the vibrations in me. My way of healing manifested itself always through a simple encounter resulting in very fine vibrations. These vibrations collected the painful flutterings from the person watching me. I opened the paths to the energies of the Universe with my simplicity, sincerity and benevolence in order that this oerson, as a rule, experiences a movement towards the bettering of his/her situation. Thus were also created the first words of this book, shyly, page by page, as guidelines to an individual and as a part of me directed to the sole objective: to help.

During my work through many years, with various types of individuals, I always followed the wishes of others, I respected their desires, listened for the quiet sobbings of all those who were not able to find a solution and created a row of rules I followed and was successful in my work. The professional people defined my ability as healing by energy therapy—in other words, with my ability to activate the energy field of any individual I add thereto my positive field and in that way, balancing over invisible uneveness and disproportions, I am able to bring the bettering of a situation. As my therapic method is neither bioenergy nor reiki, nor any other similar technique, the person I am healing should not necessarily be within a touching distance.

In this „Book of Hapiness" energy I send through it is one of its essential elements but there are other parts, not less important—parts of yourselves. Along with this Book you will be able to create your new world, it will be easier to penetrate into certain difficult situations, canalise your wishes and dreams towards the way of realisation, free yourselves from the sadness and bad luck, heal . . .

And, finally, the purpose of this Book of Hapiness has never been to make money for you must admit that I would make much more if all of you would come to me—my only wish is to bring help to everyone who is in such need and doesn't know that there is so much one can do by oneself alone.

HOW TO USE THIS BOOK

There are several acceptable ways to use this specific book. Above all this is the book which by simply entering your life will bring with itself good vibrations blocking those negative energies around you you are fighting right now, at the moment we speak. Even if you would never open this book, even of you never read a single letter in it, some difficult situations in your life will become more bearable.

My recommendation is to, before studying it and before starting to complete it, make a list of all your darkest problems as well as a list of your bravest wishes and/or objectives. For this purpose the book itself offers a space. Don't be shy—this book is meant only for you and its strength lies in my energy directed to you and you alone. This energy you cannot and may not share with anyone else.

So, you see, this is something which is yours only and will be of service whenever you need any kind of help.

„The Book of Hapiness" is not typical literature, a book you will read once and put in your shelf in order to collect dust for years to come. It is not good, it is not even easy to put it away for in that way you do not only throw some paper away—you are throwing away a part of you and a part of me.

You should have this Book of Hapiness always on you so that it may help you with its energy in situations when you are sad, weak, sick, left, frightened itd. Don't forget—the mere fact that you possess this book means a great step toward the bettering of your circumstances. You can reflect on it, it may motivate you for deeper understanding, you can write in it, by simply looking at it you can breathe in its energy, it will never stop to radiate—even after I am no more.

The book is divided in several chapters, each filled with benevolent energy by a special method—energised by my personal energy. Do not neglect the empty pages in different colours, they are important for mere observation and peaceful reflecting over this open pages which at the first glance would seem empty, will bring a part of the strength of the Universum into you and your wishes will start to realise.

After each of these coloured pages is a free space which you will complete, according to instructions, with what is needed.

My photographs may help too, they are here in order to gve you the possibility to connect with me without being dependent on telephone or the necessity an inteview.

Page of the hardest difficulties and problems we are confronted with

*"I never saw beautiful foundations—foundations are
always mud, concrete and mortar . . ."*
B. Innmon

_____
_____
_____
_____
_____
_____
_____
_____
_____
_____
_____
_____
_____
_____
_____
_____
_____
_____
_____
_____
_____
_____
_____
_____
_____
_____
_____

Page concerning wishes and goals

> *"Put onyl the goal of your life on paper. Now that we have it,*
> *black on white, we may even achieve something.*
> *There are not many who are able to determine their goal, let*
> *alone achieve it. You will not find your hapiness*
> *unless your goal isclear and always on your mind."*
>
> *Ross Byron*

Angels for Hope

GRATIFICATION

I am publishing my BOOK OF HAPPINESS with great respect for every person who ever was in contact with me for it is only in this way that I was able to be aware of the energy I possess and which I learned to focus and canalise in order to help in solving human difficulties.

Of course my thanks go to the Universum as well thanking it for the positive energy it presented me with for without this impulse I would not know how to express and render help and advice to others.

Last, but not least, I would like to offer my thanks to the members of my family who shared with me all my worries and difficulties of this activity.

Maja Panic

In order to achieve an inner peace we do not need anybody to hold our hand but only a good recipe realising such silence which may enable us for further successful steps in life.

In order to achieve an inner peace we must cross, together, three phases:

- *The phase of absolution and forgiveness;*
- *The phase of gratification; and*
- *The phase of prayer*

Absolution and Forgiveness

> *"When we are deeply wounded, we can recover only after we have forgiven."*
> *Alan Patton*

Absolution and forgiveness find its foundations in the roots of faith where absolution is always stressed as the remedy for every sin and suffering. Remeber the Bible and the Sacrament of Confession as well as the power of Jesus to absolve his disciples of sin when he said to them—"As my Father sent me—so I am sending you . . .", continuing "for those who absolve sins, the sins will be absolved for themselves" (Gospel after John) and continuing to Peter "and whatever you absolve on Earth it will also be absolved in Heaven" (Gospel after Matthew). However, in order not to connect my words to the Bible alone and its so widely described topics of forgiveness I would like to remind you how this topic is deeply, culturologically bred into every one of us, only we are not, perhaps, fully aware of it. This permanent or long-termed connection with pain we suffered by the hands of another human being injures us deeply and painfully, disturbing our inner body, bringing the mental and, sometimes, even physical pain. Absolution, forgiveness does not wipe the sin out it directs us to a better and more appropriate way, the only way which may lead us to our personal happiness.

The moment when we meet our mind, aware of our feelings in turmoil over a situation, we experience a great discrepancy. Pain is only a manifestation belongingto this chaos.

Numerous times we heard how important it is to absolve someone of the pain caused to us. If we think about it a little more, we shall establish as a fact that there were many times when we ourselves had the opportunity to render advice trying to bring one to the quickest path of recovery after such an injury—the path of absolution and forgiveness. In order to achieve peace and to achieve the first step to our wholeness we should collect all our painful and deceived expectations, calm down the tempest in our hearts and try to recognize other characteristics as well, not only the negative ones, of the person who hurt us. However, this awareness is, more often than not, not present until the moment we have cleared out the picture we have about ourselves; we often deceive ourselves with the help of the psychologically conditioned reflex of denial and supressing the things we do not like about ourselves. This perfect defensive mechanism simply deletes the data we do not like and stores them in our subconscious. Our subconscious ist not merely a deponium of unwished for and burned contents, but it constantly sends the „debris" and its contents back to us, through symbols. One of the symbolic moves of our subconscious is when the same negative characteristics we ignored in ourselves, we see in exactly the same perosn who hurt us. Then we declare for this person for whom we say that she, or he, hurt us, that we cannot and will not forgive her (or him), while we are actually, in the first place, irritated by the mirrored behaviour of ourselves in this person. By understanding this first symbolism we will be aware of some relations and injuries, will let go of these bitter feelings—and move on.

State in the following empty space persons who at the same time irritate you and who have, according to your opinion, hurt you (and why?)

_____

_____

_____

After making this list and, surely, some deep thinking, you have discoreved which part of your personality is hurt the most—but also the imperfect part of you you have to „forgive" yourself for. We shall thus separate and make us aware which of your imperfections you will, in future, not take into account in relation to other people.

According to the spiruitual principles we shall make ourselves aware—clearly and fully—of some of your imperfections—so stop a bit and wruite them down

_____
_____
_____

Although you are, by now, a bit disappointed with yourself, you have no right for this, try to feel love for yourself, such imperfect individual as you are. Forgive yourself a lot, like i.e. because in a certain situation you did not proceed differently, or try to feel compassion, forgivenes and big emotions for yourself. Remind yourself of the fact that this unhappy and frightened being within you is now growing up, starts to be aware of its ignorance but goes bravely on, is raising its head again and making way for new experiences.

The Prayer

"A soul without a prayer
is a soul without a home"
Robin A. Herchel

We all know what is a prayer—a religious act voicing a certain text where the faithful person turns to God with his/her wishes and gratitude or in just a normal conversation.

Numerous evidence has been brought till today proving the efficiency of a prayer but I selected among them one proof with scientifc basis.

In America lived and worked a scientist, N.J. Stowel by name, by his standpoints in life a through and through ateist, filled, besides, with cynism, persisting in his allegation that God is nothing but a thought, a simple idea people have. Nobody could dissuade him in this belief. However, when working in a pathological laboratory, in one clinic regarding his study concerning the research on the impulses and occurences in human brain at the moment when life changes into death, he came upon new notions and concepts.

A scientific experiment of unusual name and area was the reason for his participation in an investigation for the benefit of a very seriously ill patient with a terminal form of brain cancer. Seeing the really difficult state the patient was in, dr. Stowel and his colleagues were raedy for a final outcome at any time. They put into her room a sort of a measuring device which should have measured the occurences in her brain during the last moments of her life as well as in the moment of her death. The device had an indicator, put on zero, with the possibility to move for 500 grades to the left (positive) or 500 grades to the right (negative). As they were waiting nearby and listening, the medical scientific team heard suddenly how the patient was praying, turning to God with such a strong and loud voice that they wondered. Not long thereafter they saw that the indicator of their device moved all the way up to the maximum, 500 grades to the left (positive). It was a scienitfc shock. The brain of the dying woman connected with God and developed the highest possible grade of the positive energy.

Not long thereafter they connected the same device to a patient who was anrgy with everybody, even with God Himself. His swearings and cursings of God resulted with the movement of the indicator all the way to the right, also to the maximum, manifesting the negative force, the negative energy. Dr. N.J. Stowel declared that „ we undisputably proved, in a scentific way, the existence of a good and bad energy or forces. At that moment my ateistic standpoints weakened and I became aware how futile and stupid was my disbelief."

Thus, after the confession and great discovery of a recognized and respected medical doctor and scientist, nobody would dare to say that the prayer cannot bring you salvation. Of course the prayer presupposes peace and serenity in our soul, do not forget that each and every prayer demands our contribution through love, respect and gratitude towards the Universum. Do not give up if an answer does not arrive immediately after your prayer, it is always possible that you are not in full harmony with the energies of the Universum or that you need time to realise whatever you prayed for. The confirmation will come in the form of new life opportunities.

Select your own prayers as well as the time when you will express your deep and sincere feelings and wishes coming from your heart. Try to be humble and very concentrated, direct your spiritual being for this is the only way to make our prayers efficient and to make the fruit of our prayers create wonders in our life.

Gratifications

Time flows through our life like a torrent without giving us enough time to stop and see that we easily achieved our goals on this life path. We do not feel any relief owing to this fact nor do we consider the circumstances which were not that bad but accept and take all benefits quickly, everything goes by almost without leaving a trace of taste and smell. We shall loose the most beauties of life in vain unless we finally admit and understand events or people who went through our lives, making it richer and giving us relief, enjoyment, satisfaction, happiness or easiness. Imagine how many times somebody sent us a smile, somebody told us, at the right moment, a gentle and kind word. Have you ever in such moments given the fact a thought how many rude ungratefulness was in you and how much of good energies the Universum sent you, you broke? You were accepting all these energies as normal everyday thing. It is possible that you did not even understand what are the blessings of life at all; it is possible that some of you, in everything they do, do not feel any gratitude, neither for their good health, nor for the life itself, nor for the beauty they live. Such persons loose, owing to their character, important and good contacts with the Universum, they loose those good and fine vibrations which may prolong good moments making life even richer and better. All in all most of you who have never felt the necessity of gratitude are most probably now experiencing, according to some unwritten rule, bad things in life, withot recognizing the earlier existence of stronger energies which reward but also punish all those who felt no awareness of their behaviour nor any towards life. Such persons—and I hope there are not many among you—are today rather poor im the material sense of the word, mentally disturbed and, most probably, of bad health. As the flame of gratitude is still not distinguished in you it should motivate you, give you new strength in connection with your wishes and goals. It is possible that such people lost a lot of time till now convinced that happiness and satisfaction they are experiencing cannot be a part of their life but, believe me, little changes, more of your inner self than your outside behaviour, deep there in you, may bring large and positive changes. We have all tailored our reality according to our patterns where our inner being did not establish order and peace and thus almost nothing will manifest itself as good circumstance in life.

Thus it is your next task to awake the gratitude in yourself to the Universum for life itself, gratitude for whatever was given to you without putting up any conditions.

Write in the empty space all the good things in life you experienced and accepted „as normal everyday thing" and state below your gratitude for whatever you have. This time the number of times you say that you feel grateful is not irrelevant, there must be neither more nor less than 21, written and felt during 21 days (You may write all of them at once, but you must start and end this whithin 21 day).

i.e.
1.   *I have a wonderful family*
1.   *I thank for my wonderful family*

1.   _____
2.   _____
3.   _____
4.   _____
5.   _____
6.   _____
7.   _____
8.   _____
9.   _____
10. _____
11. _____
12. _____
13. _____
14. _____
15. _____
16. _____
17. _____
18. _____
19. _____
20. _____
21. _____

After these first three phases, without turning back to the previous pages, complete the space below with thoughts now appearing in you and, of course, your feelings.

_____
_____
_____
_____
_____
_____
_____
_____
_____
_____

When you have finished with these reflections compare this situation with the situation you entered on the first day of the book. Have you felt that you are now even slightly better? I feel your smile. . . .

But let us continue.

Happiness

There is a truth in people, not everybody around us is unhappy, on the contrary, there are a lot of people who are happy. Those lucky ones do not look as most of us imagine them—they are not people who will astonish us with their physical appearance, they are not fabulously rich nor are they full of blessings in the material sense of the word, they are not the beauties from the front pages of magazines . . . . They are those rare ones to whom the life gave enough of mind and reason as well as other virtues so that they were successful to grab whatever we think that we have been cheated of.

It is rather difficult to define happiness. Alois Vojtjecjh Smilovsky said: „After all I would have caught happiness, only if I knew what exactly it is." This is true for neither the psychological intepretations agree nor are they acceptable for every single indivdual. All hitherto suggested definitions include health, freedom, material goods, inner peace and similar. One of the definition of happiness also says that happiness lies with a permanent positive emotional situation including peaceful satisfaction with one's life but also the active satisfaction resulting from various achievements.

As I would not paraphrase further on this and in order to spare you reading phrases you heard many times before and which never helped in solving your problems, let us take a break now, take one moment which will later show to have been crucial for you.

Think a bit and determine your personal definition of happiness.

_____

_____

_____

_____

_____

_____

_____

_____

_____

_____

After defining your happiness yourself it is time to achieve this state of your consciousness, to feel powerful for you really can achieve this. Go to a quiet place or to a quiet corner of your home. Connect with me through one of my photographs and feel how you are not alone in realising your happiness (to which you have a full right). The time when you are going to do this is absolutely irrelevant.

After you have fully quieted down fill the next 49 rows by writing every time „I am happy". In the second row write down the thought which automatically blocks you in this feeling.

1. I am happy
1. . . . . (i.e. why was it necessary for me to receive a notice at work?)

1. _____
2. _____
3. _____
4. _____
5. _____
6. _____
7. _____
8. _____
9. _____
10. _____
11. _____
12. _____
13. _____
14. _____
15. _____
16. _____
17. _____
18. _____
19. _____
20. _____
21. _____
22. _____
23. _____
24. _____
25. _____

26. _____
27. _____
28. _____
29. _____
30. _____
31. _____
32. _____
33. _____
34. _____
35. _____
36. _____
37. _____
38. _____
39. _____
40. _____
41. _____
42. _____
43. _____
44. _____
45. _____
46. _____
47. _____
48. _____
49. _____

In the next step choose ten largest hindrances hindering you in achieving your happiness.

_____
_____
_____
_____
_____
_____
_____
_____
_____

We shall now approach the solutions of these hindrances

Select your hindrances and problems so that we may get a scheme as a plan of our actions. This is necessary as none of the difficulties and problems you are confronted with came at once and thus it cannot dissappear at once as well.

Easy solved hindrances	Difficult to solve hindrances on	Hindrances depending other opersons
_____	_____	_____
_____	_____	_____
_____	_____	_____
_____	_____	_____

After this classification has been done, arrange the hindrances according to their solving priorities, while all hindrances which, at this moment, depend on other persons simply cross from your list. We are working here in order to change the things only you can change, depending exclusively on you, while all you need is a little wind in your back.

_____
_____
_____
_____
_____
_____
_____
_____
_____

All that we need now is to approach and solve one problem at a time.

The only thing you need to do in the days that follow is to combine our energies and focus thus on solving the problem. In order to trigger off our energies to work for your benefit every day, till the problem is solved, we shall connect through the photograph and through the colour—you will meditate and repeat, forty nine times, the sentence—I wish to solve . . . . repeating this until you have solved that particular problem.

You will, as I said, name and point the problem out on the page foreseen for it, write down the date and an objectively stated time period within which you intend to solve that particular problem (time period for problem solving is, objectively, 49 days). The remaining empty space use for entering short notes. It is possible that during the time dedicated to finding the solution you may also receive a hidden message or suggestion, or that yu will simply have an idea how to help yourself. This page is also foreseen for writing down any peculiar circumstance speaking in your favour when getting the problem solved.

Warning: you cannot start with the next problem until you have solved the previous one.

1. Problem / difficulty / hindrance to the achievement of your personal happiness

   _____

   _____

   Problem solving starting date:

   Space for your personal notes:

2. Problem / difficulty /hindrance to the achievement of your personal happiness

    _____

    _____

    Problem solving starting date:

    Space for yur personal notes:

3. Problem / difficulty/ hindrance to the achievement of your personal happiness

    _____

    _____

    Problem solving starting date:

    Space for your personal notes:

4. Problem (dfficulty/ hindrance to the achievement f your personal happiness

_____

_____

Problem solving starting date:

Spacefor your personal notes:

5. Problem / difficulty / hindrance to the achievment of your personal happiness

   _____

   _____

   Problem solving starting date:

   Space for your personal notes:

RED

6. Problem / difficulty / hindrance to the achievment of your personal happiness

_____

_____

Problem solving starting date:

Space for your personal notes:

7. Problem / difficulty / hindrance to the achievement of your personal happiness

    _____

    _____

    Problem solving starting date:

    Space for your personal notes:

8. Problem / difficulty /hindrance to the achievment of your personal happiness

   _____

   _____

   Problem solving starting date:

   Space for your personal notes:

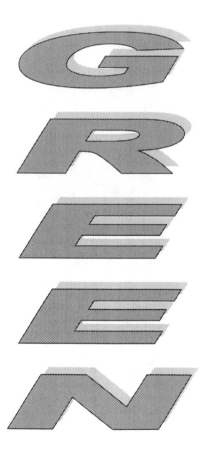

9. Problem / difficulty / hindrance to the achievement of your personal happiness

_____

_____

Problem solving starting date:

Space for your personal notes:

PURPLE

10. Problem / difficulty / hindrance to the achievement of your personal happiness

_____

_____

Problem solving starting date:

Space for your personal notes:

TASKS REPRESENTING YOUR PLEDGE FOR THE FUTURE HAPPINESS, SATISFACTION AND HEALTH IN YOUR LIFE

This book would not have been so successful when it would not contain, besides my energy, all the coming positive changes in you. After implementing the previous actions and after studying this Book of Happiness and after taking your first steps toward awareness regarding the problematic situations, I presume that, today, you have already become a more satisfied person.

We are now approaching the primeval change of your standpoints in life, making your life better, in every sense of the word. If you have hitherto respected the laws and principles as sugegsted below, continue in the same way, just enter more awareness in everything you do and think. If some of the things from the further chapters are only barely familiar or if you have been taught them as a small child, it is high time to accept these things now as an integral part of your thoughts, life movements, standpoints and principles.

Of course, in accordance with my hitherto work and activity and my principle that small wonders happen only within certain figures, I selected 21 life principles for you to be adopted during 21 weeks. Regarding you yourself and the flow of good vibrations which are at your disposal, it will not be easy to bring some of the things to your awareness and it would be the best to try and achieve this slowly, by selecting, with care, the time and the rhytm which suits you best.

So study the principle offered, and write down, at the end of the page, the date you have adopted it for your lifetime.

Adopt the principles slowly, the best would be one every week, returning to it every now and then in order to write down, in the empty space, the positive events which will follow very quickly after the principle has been adopted.

THE FIRST LIFE PRINCIPLE
THE FORCE OF THE MIND AND THE THOUGHT

From that moment you should start to be open for the first and, at the same time, basic principle of life showing that exactly the matter from your thoughts is actually the energy by which you seek and accept everything the Universum wants to give you anyway. Namely, all your thoughts, wishes, visions, beliefs, optimism, pessimism, your yearnings . . . . all this represents your life. From today onwards your thoughts will be decisive, happy, sincere, fair and dedicated to every single thing from your enviroment. In order to achieve such beautiful thoughts you should also be aware of the fact that the control over your own thoughts is the assumption for good things to start to happen. Thoughts are a great and strong creative force attracting familiar energies!

Date the first Principle of Life has been adopted
_____

Notes

THE SECOND LIFE PRINCIPLE
WHATEVER I GIVE I WILL ALSO RECEIVE

The second Principle of Life has been familiar to your from those long ago days when our parents were educating us, for this is only one of the common wise sayings which we will find in every religion throughout the world. It is not difficult to understand that we also do not want to be victims of anybody's negative activity, nor do we wish to live without that wonderfu feeling—happiness. The problem arises only when we ourselves must undertake some activities in order to get what we want.

Thus, try to be, for a slight nuance, different from this day onwards: instead of all you have hitherto offered to your friends, family, colleagues, neighbours—start to be expressively benevolent, outcoming, kind, caring and warm. It is not difficult to make this principle work, even if you feel that is is not easy to do so. There are always ways and opportunities for a nice word and a smile.

Date the second Principle of Life has been adopted

_____

Notes

THE THIRD LIFE PRINCIPLE
INNER PEACE

A very important fact in your life is surely the possibiity to achieve an inner peace—an excellence very few people are able to boast with. If you are often burdened with all sorts of things, disconsolate, angry, pathetic and similar, you must know that with feelings like these there simply are no happy circumstances. Good balance and focussing on life itself smothers all sorts of spiritual restlessness spending othewise huge quantities of our potential positive energy and thus we stay, all the time, as a habit, full of worries, problems, various dissatisfactions, entering the ominous maelstrom of undesirable life events.

From now on your thoughts must carry a strong desire, followed by proper breathing (light breathing in, grey breathing out) to establish control with the sole goal to establish the inner peace.

Date the third Principal of lIfe was adopted

_____

Notes

THE FOURHT LIFE PRINCIPLE
IT IS ABSOLUTELY ENOUGH JUST TO LISTEN

Most of the partnership relations, deep friendships, blood relations, brother—and sisterhoods and dedicated partnerhoods break up only for the reason that people do not listen and wish only to present their own mental situations. Thus those poor ones who are not listened to and want to present their own problems and troubles, often, after numerous unsuccessful attempts, raise their voice at last with a statement which, as a rule hurts and offends us. This is, approximately, how every chaos and breakup in relationships ocurs.

Good relationships should be nursed and situations where you are always ending up as the main speaker, the wisest of all and the most important one who always has something clever to say should be skillfully avoided.

Of course, to listen to somebody who is presenting own worries and troubles, who wants to entrust us with a secret, who ist thinking aloud—is not easy. Listening to others needs concentration and absolute attention in order to observe and grasp all facts we did no seet at the first glance. The reward to a good listener will, in the first place, be the pleasant feeling one gets by such behaviour from the person one has listened to, gratitude on his/her face but also wisdom we may acquire by listening to others. Next to this is also respect and popularity on the side of the ones who have been listened to—what more can one wish for!

Date the fourth Principle of Life was adopted

_____

Notes

THE FIFTH PRINCIPLE OF LIFE
GETTING HUMBLE

You have many contacts and, surely there are some people from your environment you approach with a feeling of, more or less, contempt. I surely do not have to remind you how many times in your life were you rudely proud and arrogant with some, by your opinion, „common" people. Go on, try to remeber some of the behaviour you are ashamed of.

_____

_____

_____

Dont't feel embarassed now any more; already after you have achieved awareness regarding such events you have adopted the 5th Principleof Life ordering you to change yourbehaviour against others. Try, for a change, to be humble, exclude, permanently, your strong ego in order to find out how much understanding is there in your heart for others. As more patience you will show, as well as tolerace, love and gentleness, but also understanding for the problems of others, that much more will you also receive. This humbleness will make you start with a fully new behaviour without that false and horrible ego which is squatting in your inner self, making all sorts of troubles for you.

Date the fifth Principle of Life was adopted

_____

Notes

THE SIXTH PRINCIPLE OF LIFE
PLANNING

There are numerous published handbooks basing every good theory on the importance of planning in life. When I was tending this life principle I was convinced myself about the efficiency of it and thus I strongly recommend that it is very necessary to take the fact into consideration that planning your life is the half step to a full success. Somebody clever said: „ You won't know how to reach your destination if you do not know what this destination is!"

Don't make only short-termed plans in order to cover up old problems. Give yourself time to work out carefully and in full detail your life plan entering into it all the smaller steps necessary for the realisation of big goals. Age, the level of your education, economy situation, your marital status . . . . all this is not important.

Do not forget that the success of your plan surely depends on how determined you are to bring a goal or an idea to the end.

Date the sixth Principle of Life was adopted

_____

Notes

THE SEVENTH PRINCIPLE OF LIFE
DEDICATION

This Principle of Life speaks about dedication—word you will hardly understand at first glance for we use it rarely. Some translations are precise enough, interpreting dedication as an enthusiasm, being filled up with good energies . . . . I would, however, describe it as a feeling located somewhere deep within us, a feeling necessary for the realisation of every step, a feeling we need whenever we decide to do something and whenever we feel to be alive. There is no way to enter happiness or joy into our lives without this enthusiasm, without this passion.

At every moment from today try to do things with dedication, be enchanted with its beauty and possibilities standing in front of you.

Dedication is the way where all good vibrations open up and the potential of good things will grow into something very concrete.

Date the seventh Principle of Life was adopted

_____

Notes

THE EIGHTH PRINCIPLE OF LIFE
ENDLESS GIVING

There is a great possibility that you have not thrown this Principle of Life out from your own life, however, I am sure that we can do even better and give more, give „that certain something" from us.

I also know that a great truth lies in the thoughts that are going through your head now:giving, giving, giving and never expecting something in return . . . ! Why? What is the point? Howe long? I admit there is some truth in that too. Only, every time you have given something sincerely your energy, like a boomerang, returns straight to you, bringing you gifts straight from the Universum itself.

Gving—giving from the bottom of your heart—simply brings luck and along with it productivity in every sense of the word. Endure in this life principle much longer than a few times as was hitherto your practice.

Date the eighth Principle of Life was adopted

_____

Notes

THE NINETH PRINCIPLE OF LIFE
LOVE INSTEAD OF HATE

Love is always afirmation of the Universal energy flowing through and causes motivation and exceptionally good forces of life. This flow-through can be destroyed (with permanent and irreversible consequences) by the feeling of hate formed sometimes in rage, sometimes in anger, worry, sorrow . . . . Hate changes the life circumstances, unfortunately for the worse and now is the exact moment to exchange this bitter feeling, if you have it in yourself, permanently, with something else; freedom and noble characteristics. Only at the moment when you have freed yourself from hate you will be able to control yourself and your life, bring correct decisions and the Universal energy will reward you with security, health and fruit of good life.

Date the nineth Principle of Life was adopted
_____

Notes

THE TENTH PRINCIPLE OF LIFE
HONESTY

Many books were written about human honesty and manyy wise proverbs were said. Some of them you may recognize among these contents in order to refresh some blazed trails of good human behaviour. A sincere self-analysis on this level will show you a sad fact, namely, that you yourself have been at least several times in your life dishonest. Deliberations you used in some certain situations is surely justified with the allegation that skill of a rational mind and wise words bring the human progress but one one should always also look for a deeper meaning of our thoughts and words. Dishonesty, which is often a faithful follower reflects, actually, your character, your nature and this nature formes then your (horrible) world. It is of utmost importance to be honest in every possible situation, regardless of what we do or say when we mean the best for our life. How many times have you forgotten to be honest in regard to others and then wondered why when some, not foreseen circumstances, turned against you?

Date the tenth Principle of Life was adopted

_____

Notes

THE ELEVENTH PRINCIPLE OF LIFE
DO NOT JUDGE

Already since the time of the Bible judging was a word wise people avoided not wishing to cause the anger of God or the Universum. Today we react very easily letting our anger to bring us to a throne wherefrom we feel free to judge others. Who and what gives us the right to bring judgement abut others? Such behaviour cannot, by any spiritual or natural law, bring blessings to your life! Every time when we behave in that manner we loose a part of ourselves for not respecting spiritual laws. This part sends us then messages through the Universum in the form of undesirable vibrations.

Think and remind yourself of the situations when you blamed and judged mercilessly and then enter with this empty space a few sincere judgments concerning yourself. Try to be objective and sincere!

_____

_____

_____

_____

_____

I believe that now you have started to form your new destiny „moulding" your character so that it may direct you in the future to state loudly and clearly recommendations and the judgement, even if it does enter your mind, lay somewhere aside.

Date the eleventh Principle of Life was adoted

_____

Notes

THE TWELFTH PRINCIPLE OF LIFE
FRIENDSHIP

Not all lectures in the world nor all wonderful statements about love can often leave the desired impact in us. Love is one thing and friendship is richness which, when it is strong, becomes a very powerful pact winning over any hindrance. Acting on the basis of a friendhsip brings in its finality only a never ending goodness. Good friendship means satisfaction. Satisfaction attracts positive energy; positive energy brings joy and happiness as well as recovery and comfort. But not the strongest friendship may endure if there is no confidence and if we easily waive our friends because of their mistakes or faults, because of their physical appearance, their material status or similar. To have a real friendship means knowing how to keep it and care for it regardless of the distances and other circumstances, to have friendship means to be rich and happy.

Date the twelfth Principle of Life was adopted

_____

Notes

THE THIRTEENTH PRINCIPLE OF LIFE
DESTROY THE GREED IN YOU

Greed is an evil and negative energy bringing only damage to our life. It is only our heavy burden arising from too great desires and egotism we carry in ourselves. Keeping everyrthing for you and you alone is the way to create, sooner or later, your own personal hell where you will soon need the help of other sins and vices in order to combat your conscience which will surely bother you here and then.

Greed is traditionally put uder the category of the „deadly sins", bringing you, without fail, to a path of suffering and pain, disappointment and surrendering to lust. In order to combat greed you must become moderate, you must smother every rage in you—but destroying rage is anyway our next Principle of Life.

Date the thirteenth Principle of life was adopted
_____

Notes

THE FOURTEENTH PRINCIPLE OF LIFE
CONTROLING YOUR RAGE

The perceptions of the daily events provoke often emotions known under the term—rage. Rage is a very strong emotion destroying, as a rule, every love, bringing destruction to our mind and body but also to everything surrounding us. Rage definitey destroys the potential of happiness and satisfaction.

Every time when you have been brought in the state of rage you are risking your body and soul for you open the paths to hidden and deadly sicknesses which will later develop in you accepting at that moment destructible and often wild behaviour. Every time we let the rage out, we concentrate thus in ourselves great quantities of negative energy and it is only logical that nothing good can be expected of it.

A furious person and his/her furious outbursts destroy pride and self-respect and life becomes meaningless and limited. With letting ourselves to the rage we start a very dangerous merry-go-round instead of facing things, persons and events provoking rage in us.

Write in the empty space 5 situations which awake the dangerous beast in you and control each day this ugly emotion. Never forget that rage is a hidden emotion and that you will be the first one to be wounded by its bloody jaws and only thereafter those who, by your subjective way, deserve this.

Date the fourteenth Principle of Life was adopted

_____

Notes

THE FIFTEENTH PRINCIPLE OF LIFE
MATERIAL ORDER

The journey towards a happy life looses often the guideline concerning a big and obvious problem suffered by most—the material chaos. What kind of pictures and emotions flow through your thoughts when you start to think about your material existence, the issues concerning real estate and cash, debts and non-paid bills.

Spirituality is an everyday necessity but our different interests and standpoints often bring us into hopeless situations, creating in us despair and not letting us free ourselves from everything. Life filled with the fight for material things destroys all our mental, emotional, even physical potentials. You have probably forgotten to think, feel, listen, touch . . . . without seeing in the background a horror movie of financial problems smothering every help from the Universum. If you really want to be educated spiritually, if you really want to feel happiness and satisfaction, you must introduce order, work and discipline in the process of living in the material world as well. I maintain that without the visible material matter there will be no invisible spiritual matter either. A hungry person who is cold cannot complete this book and think about a better tomorrow. Your material problems and a material basis for for a happy life you must provide for yourself. A good basis, product of rational thinking, will bring you into a situation where you will have clean and correct thoughts and such thoughts will very quickly return the same cleanliness in this field as well.

Listen to my advice, determine your priorities in the material matter and issues, make your personal table of things you cannt go wihout regarding your existence, determine priorities for various payments and start, only then, full of joy and optimistic, to think of the ways how to solve this. Concentration will help in every further step oft his way. Do not forget that the intensity of the problem is not decisive fact for your success—the decisive fact is you facing this and your faith, care and positive standpoint will smother negative energies opening the door to the energy of the Universum which is always positive and, after all, on time.

The date the fifteenth Principle of Life was adopted

_____

Notes

THE SIXTEENTH PRINCIPLE OF LIFE
HEALTH IS MOST IMPORTANT

All we have been talking about hitherto and all what stayed unfinished between us wouldn't have any sense at all without your good health. The more realiable and positive energy you are surely feeling now in yourself will fill your body, your mind and your soul on your way to recovery or on the way to keep yourself healthy. If, inspite of everything you have hitherto been lucky and your health has not been seriously endangered, consider this as a true gift from the Universum. Try to accept this principle of life ordering you to shine in the future and spread joy expressing gratitude, wehenever the opportunity, for your good health.

Persons who have hitherto been ill, had serious or less serious medical problems, will acquire, when working on themselves, a new characteristic: courage using it to face all health problems. Energetic circumstances are submitted, as everything inthe world, to change: Universum has its own dimension, levels and perceptions and its strength will widen our ranges and enable our recovery.

Date the fifteenth Priciple of Life was adopted

_____

Notes

THE SEVENTEENTH PRINCIPLE OF LIFE
APPEARANCE

Although you are aware of the fact that the world around us is nothing but an illusion it is probable that you are not satisfied with your appearance. In such moments one should think very positively for a clear reasoning of such situation can lead you to two directions.

One is your external appearance which does not answer your expectations but the appearance is, in a higher level of consideration, only an experience of your mind. All yur bodily wishes and situations of your soul are reflected in your body and face. If you are strong enough to use the whole bias of the Universum leaving its doors wide open for you, step bravely in and care for your other virtues, calm down and concentrate. Ony then will you be able to see how your external appearance is suddenly changing. Your beauty was hidden in the shadow of various bitter feelings you were filled with till now. Try to enrich your external appearance with a part of your soul and in a moment you will see that your appearace, your beauty, can rise in its illusory reality.

The second solution is only a supplement to the first one for, if you have mastered the external circumstances in your life, if you apply the above principles of life, you will most probably take a standpoint of a permanent interest with the purpose to render an even greater effort in order to promote your appearance.

Date the seventeenth Principle of Life was adopted

_____

Notes

THE EIGHTEENTH PRINCIPLE OF LIFE
USE YOUR WILL

All our life tasks and choices depend to a great extent on the nature of our thoughts; these thoughts are restricted, determined, pushed, smothered, stopped and motivated by them. Thank to our personal will each and every one of us has the opportunity to reach extraordinary results in each of the fields of life. The will which we have, or have not, determines, finally, your world. If you have the will to put order into your life, you will find the way; the will itself will find a path so that good energies may reach you. Today is the day you will accept this pprinciple of life and develop our possibilities. Today is the day when you will rather do nothing then apply only half of your will. Everything you are going to do in the future will be in most part based on your strenghtened decision, on your will!

Date this eighteenth Principle of Life was adopted

_____

Notes

THE NINETEENTH PRINCIPLE OF LIFE
SMOTHERING IDLENESS

Idleness is one of the characterstics we often meet inthe English romantic novels suggesting always that out of idleness an, at least, ugly scene will be born. Exactly this often decsribed feeling of a disturbed consciunsness kills very quickly all inner potentials throwing us to the bottom of all ethical scales. Activities are being smothered, bad habits are acquired, bleak thoughts are entering, good energy is destroyed. By destroying good energy you also destroy your body and your mind and all this results, of course, with the loss of every meaning. This principle of life orders you to be productive, have a glowing wish for life, directing your body and mind not to submit to any negative energies through your negative thoughts teaching you how to avoid painful situations in life.

Date the nineteenth Principle of Life was adopted

_____

Note

THE TWENTIETH PRINCIPLE OF LIFE
SMILES AND LAUGHTER

The effect of laughter and smiles was also numerous times described and ascribed to everything which may bring happiness into life. The medical phenomenon regardig our blood circuation under these circumstances I will not enter into this time for I am sure that most of you are aware of the fact that laughter is the best medicine, stronger than any magic, more serious than any path, smile helps us to realise all our wishes. The energy circulating through our body and mind is fully natural and positive when we round it up with a smile as the finest frame ever. Smile as well as laughter costs nothing, it is natural and inborn, only cramps in our face are something unnatural. This is exactly the reason why you should melt this gift of nature with the good vibrations of the Universum in order to move your body and your soul acquiering thus a great benefit for your life.

Date the twentieth Principle of Life was adopted
_____

Notes

THE TWENTYFIRST PRINCIPLE OF LIFE
THROWING STRESS AWAY

Stress was, of course, so many times researched and described by various media that it is senseless to search for anything new in this respect. Under the term stress we understand today everything which provokes bad emotions: sadness, jelaousy, rage, sorrow etc. There is no unique formulae by which one could remove stress full from our lives in full but surely there shouldn't be that much stress as you often feel. It is my personal belief that we are able to control every emotional thunder following stress by numerous methods suggested by medical doctors, scientists, healers and other spiritual leaders. A very effective method in controlling stress is surely enlightened truth regarding the damages this energy may create, putting the accent on the soul smothering in the sick body. The body is considered as sick exactly at the moment we feel the shiverings caused by stress.

Empty space in this place will be useful only if you write down what can (most often) cause stress in you and what will you try to change, very soon, in order to control stress you have hitherto so much been exposed to.

Date the twentyfirst Principle of Life was adopted

_____

Notes

THERAPY BY COLOURS

(The text used here is taken from the book *Introduction to the Magic of Helping Yourself* by Maja Panic)

Light is a mask of the Universum, of the Creator. The complete life on Earth depends on the energy of light—rays of sun, the source of life and energy as such. Colour is a different quality of light and may be a male (positive) or a female (negative) force. Soul lives always in a colour. It needs such colour in exactly the same way as we humans need air. When we take the colour away from the light, it is as if we have lost the awareness regarding the matter. All knowledge regarding Universum is accepted through electro-magnetic radiation developing in the components of the colour energy, departing then to different parts of the body, revitalising it. Light and colours provoke chemical reactions and changes and thus is light, whose source is the energy of the sun, the strongest healing force in the Universum. Life is colour and every organ has its specific colour and each colour has its specific intelligence acting selectively and knowing its task and goal well. Colour represents a vibrating energy able to activate a certain organ, gland or system in your body. This is why the energy, as the result of the applied colour, is very important in the healing process: in order to create harmony and balance between body and mind. Such healing procedures are not only of physical but of spiritual nature as well—creating a connection between the physical body and the finer vibrations. Colour represents a bridge between the internal and the external stimuli. The personal quota of the ultraviolet light is much higher only we do not use in it full—we can surely strenghten this point by exposing our body as much as possible to the natural light.

WHERE THERE IS LIGHT—THERE IS NO DARKNESS

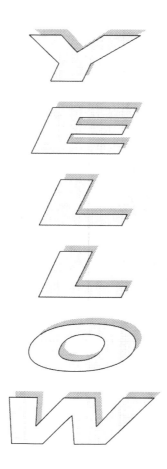

| **PRIMARY COLOURS** | **Red** | |
| | **Blue** | |

OPPOSITE COLOURS	**Red**	**Blue**
	Orange	**Indigo**
		Purple

Green is a neutral colour

COMPLEMENTARY COLOURS	**Red**	**Green**
	Yellow	**Purple**
	Orange	**Blue**

WARM COLOURS

Enforce the activity and circulation, stimulating all functions in the organism

Red is the warmest colour with the longest length of the visible spectrum
Orange the craddle oft he soul

COLD COLOURS slown down activitiy and circulation

Blue calms down, stops activity
Indigo the coldest colour and the most difficult one for visualisation
Purple the shortest wave-length in the visible spectrum

HARMONIZING COLOUR—triggers off functions

Green self-regulator, balancing effect

THE BODY OF THE RAINBOW

Body is a crystal sucking in the solar light reflecting through chakras seven rainbow colours back to the Universum. Pituitary gland is a prism breaking the energy of light, dispersing and distributing it through the body.

RED COLOUR

Red colour is alo called a great energiser or the center of vitality. This colour is warm and flaming. It disperses and opens blocked parts liberating these parts of its tension. It is excellent for the areas of rigidity and tameness.

Red colour stimulates us and connects us with the root chakra causing the andrenaline gland to secrete adrenaline. This of course results in a greater personal strength. Red colour also stimulates haemoglobine to multiply enlarging thus the energy level by rising the body temperature. It is useful when a person suffers anaemia and disturbances of blood and blood circulation.

Topic: it brings you down to earth, stability, power of will, material matter, sexuality, passion
Symbols: fire, warmth, red rose, energy, blood
Fragrant oil: cedar-tree, carnation, pine, cinnamon

Effect of red on:
- physical level: energises, brings you down to earth, strenghtens
- mental level: stimulates will and dedication, energy of change
- emotional level: passion, courage, freedom
- spiritual level: transformation

ORANGE COLOUR

Orange is the true colour of the planet Sun: it acts liberating on the mind and the body. As this is the colour of red and yellow it actually connects the physical energy with the mental wisdom bringing transformation between the lower physical reaction and higher mental response. This is exactly the reason why they sometimes call it „the ray od wisdom". The colour is warm, joyful. It can heal physical body (red) bringing at the same time larger reason in (yellow) necessary for our healing; orange colour helps the assimilation of new ideas as well as the assimilation of mental enlightenment. It increases immunity and sexual potential; it greatly helps in illness of kidneys, digestion and thorax.

Topic: sensuality, happiness, creativity, energy, sexuality, ambition, centering
Symbol: orange clothes
Stones: topaz, sapphire, quartz, ahate, calcite
Fragrant oil: sandalwood, yasmine

Effect of orange on:
- physical level: good at shock and large traumatic injuries;
- mental level: calmness, antidepressive
- emotional level: sensuality, laughter, bliss
- spiritual level: self-understanding, full dedication

PURPLE COLOUR

Purple colour is really the colour of divinity and divine spirit. It acts only at deep levels. It is mostly used for physical states and for widening our understanding of the Universum.

Topic: healing, spirituality, mental talents
Symbol: yin and yang
Stones: amethyst
Fragrant oil: incense, lotus

Effect of the purple colour on:
- physical level: calms down on all levels
- mental level: transformation
- emotional level: healing through pain and self-sacrifice
- spiritual level: meditation, spirituality

GREEN COLOUR

Green is also a healing colour used already by ancient Egyptians and Chinese. It contains physical and spiritual nature and is in full balance and harmony. Its effect is relaxing, it stimulates the heart chakra and is connected with it. The practical sense brings us to healing problems concerning blood pressure and all problematic conditions of heart.

Topic: space, harmony, physical healing
Symbol: nature, fertility
Stones: emerald, malachite, aventurin
Fragrant oil: rose oil, mint, sage, pine and cinnamon

BLUE COLOUR

As somebody already said blue colour is the most effective antiseptic in the world; it acts cooling and helps in bleeding, decreases temperature and helps with inflammations of throat. It is positive and has a definitely relaxing effect, brings in loyalty and reliability. It mostly stimulates the throat-chakra and exactly this chakra represents the primary center for expression and communication through speech. Blue may be used for disturbances connected to communication and the solarised blue colour is a good tonic for inflammation of throat.

Topic: communications, peace, wisdom
Symbol: sea, water
Stones: aquamarine, turquoise, sapphyre, blue opal
Fragrant oil: sage, lilly of the valley, yasmine, lotus

Effect of the blue colour on:
- physical level: cools, against headache, calms down
- mental level: intuition, will, objectivity
- spiritual level: iniciation, meditation, higher level of communication

INDIGO BLUE

This colur is phenomenal for cleansing the blood flow but it is also good for mental problems as it cleans and liberates. This colour contains the dark blue with a minimal quantity of red. Indigo stimulates the forehead chakra (third eye) and controls epiphysis ruling thus the physical and spiritual power of observation (clairvoyance). Indigo is the ray of the spirit.

Topic: intuition, clairvoyance, secrets
Symbol: night sky, magic
Stones: sapphyre, sodalite, lubulite
Fragrant oil: yasmine, mint

Effect of indigo on:
- physical level: decreases tension, heals headache and toothache
- mental level: clairvoyance
- emitional level: mysticism, meditation

YELLOW COLOUR

Yellow helps with nerves and increases mind abilities as with awakening the mental inspiration. It is wonderful for all conditions of the nervous system and also stimulates the solar plexus (mental center) it connects with; heals exhaustion and other serious mental states. This colour may be used with all problematic stomach conditions as well as liver and colon conditions.

Topic: intelect, bringing down mental blockades
Symbol: sunflower, Sun

Stones: topaz, yellow diamond, pirite
Fragrant oil: rosemary, cammomile, laurel, lemon, vanilla

Effect of colour on:
- physical level: skin problems, nervous and kidney problems, plexus area
- mental level: intellectual cleanliness
- emotional level: happiness, bliss
- spiritual level: enlightement, light, mind

PINK COLOUR

Pink nuances are the colours of human love, without including the sexual yearning but only including love which makes us happy. This colour has an impact on all colours in our aura, changing the human love into a spiritual force. It simply softens down forces and energies, that is, it has the power to transform all negative states in a certain situation to the better. If we add red to this colour it cleanses and if we add green, it will allow us peace and serenity. Pink is always connected with romantic feelings, good intentions, healing of emotions and care.

BLACK COLOUR

Is manifested light in the potential which may be something it has not become yet. We connect this colour with depressionm, death, sadness and black magic. As people never really understood black colour ths colour really remained hidden and mysterous till the present day. Black is not a colour—but it gives power to other colors.

Topic: self-control, discipline, truth, wisdom
Symbol; death magic sadness
Stones: black quartz, diamond
Fragrant oil: yew-tree, myrtle, basil,

BROWN COLOUR

Brown colour is connected to the mother Earth and with all stable and strong matter. This colour keeps us in the same old forms but with the necessity of certain changes and the cleansing process.

Topic: healing animals and plants, bringing decisions, strenghtening friendship

Symbols: earth, work
Stones: smoke quartz, amber, granite
Fragrant oil: birch, lilly, camphor, bergamot

GREY COLOUR

Grey is a colour of self-sacrifice and it is always connected with fear. It should always be refined with other colours in order to be cleansing. It is recommnded to use this colour as little as possible.

GOLDEN COLOUR

Golden is the strongest healing colour of all, good for healing any disease and any condition, it has a male power and strenghtens all body and spiritual energy fields. It is the colour of richness, promotion of strength and effect of the Universum. The golden ray is used for balancing the male energy.

Stones: gold, diamond, cytrin, tiger eye, carneol
Fragrant oil: patchouli, cedar-tree, cinnamon

SILVER COLOUR

This colour is used for balancing female energy with persons where undesired illnesses should be removed. It is best for healing carcinoma, tissue and blood. Besides this it is cnnected to clairvoyance, telepathy and astral energy.

Stones: silver, mountain crystal, pearl, mother-of-pearl

WHITE COLOUR

This colour is perfect for awakening the spirit; it is the light of perfection and of the Universum. By directing white colour to the aura it stimulates the divine nature and healing.

Topic: cleansiness, exchange for any other colour
Symbol: spirituality, cleanliness, angel, moon
Stones: opal, pearl, mother-of-pearl, achate
Fragrant oil: myrtle, thyme, anise, parsley

** OWING TO THE LIMITED MATERIAL NOT ALL COLOURS COULD HAVE RECEIVED THEIR OWN PAGE, HOWEVER YOU MAY CHOOSE FROM A COLOUR FROM THE ONES OFFERED WHICH SUITS YOU FOR YOUR MEDITATION AND TRY BY DEEP OBSERVATION OF THE PAGE TO RECEIVE THE HIDDEN MESSAGE WHICH MAY HELP IN SOLVING YOUR PROBLEMS.

.... to be continued